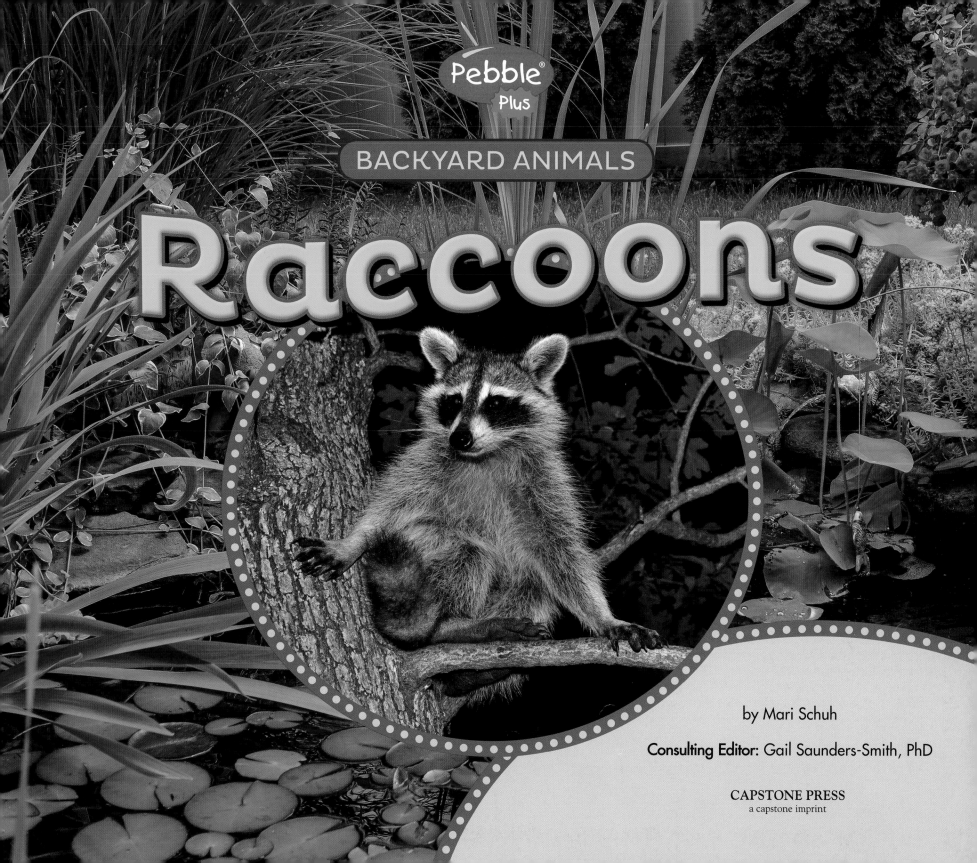

Pebble® Plus

BACKYARD ANIMALS

Raccoons

by Mari Schuh

Consulting Editor: Gail Saunders-Smith, PhD

CAPSTONE PRESS
a capstone imprint

Pebble Plus is published by Capstone Press,
1710 Roe Crest Drive, North Mankato, Minnesota 56003
www.capstonepub.com

Library of Congress Cataloging-in-Publication Data
Schuh, Mari C., 1975– author.
  Raccoons / by Mari Schuh.
pages cm. — (Pebble plus. Backyard animals)
Summary: "An introduction to raccoons, their characteristics, habitat, food, life cycle, and
threats. Includes a hands-on activity related to wildlife watching"— Provided by publisher.
  Audience: Ages 4–8.
  Audience: K to grade 3.
  Includes bibliographical references and index.
ISBN 978-1-4914-2087-4 (library binding) — ISBN 978-1-4914-2328-8 (ebook PDF)
  1. Raccoon—Juvenile literature. I. Title.
QL737.C26S38 2015
599.76'32—dc23   2014032330

Editorial Credits
Nikki Bruno Clapper, editor; Juliette Peters, designer; Tracy Cummins, media researcher;
Tori Abraham, production specialist

Photo Credits
Dreamstime: Ajones232, 7; FLPA: L Lee Rue, 17; iStockphotos: FRANKHILDEBRAND, 22 Left,
Cover; Science Source: Hans Reinhard, 15; Shutterstock: Becky Sheridan, 1, 19, Bildagentur
Zoonar GmbH, 24, Inge Schepers, 22 Right, jennyt, 21, jgorzynik, Design Element, Cover
Background, Mike Truchon, 9, Pagina, Back Cover, PinkPueblo, Design Element, Rosalie
Kreulen, 11; Thinkstock: Sam Lee, 5, Zoonar RF, 13

Note to Parents and Teachers

The Backyard Animals set supports national curriculum standards for science
related to life science and ecosystems. This book describes and illustrates
raccoons. The images support early readers in understanding the text. The
repetition of words and phrases helps early readers learn new words. This book
also introduces early readers to subject-specific vocabulary words, which are
defined in the Glossary section. Early readers may need assistance to read some
words and to use the Table of Contents, Glossary, Read More, Internet Sites,
Critical Thinking Using the Common Core, and Index sections of the book

Printed in the United States of America in Stevens Point, Wisconsin.
092014   008479WZS15

Table of Contents

Backyard Raccoons

Late at night, a creature with
a black mask looks for food.
It might be in your yard!
Raccoons are nocturnal.
They come out at night.

Raccoons are mammals
with bushy, ringed tails.
Dark masks help them hide
from enemies. Masks also
help raccoons see at night.

Raccoons weigh

10 to 30 pounds

(4.5 to 14 kilograms).

Males are bigger and

heavier than females.

Where Raccoons Live

Most raccoons live in
North or South America.
They make dens in trees,
on the ground, in barns,
and under porches.

What Raccoons Do

Raccoons eat almost anything. They munch bugs, plants, and even fish. Their long fingers can open clamshells and trash cans.

Most raccoons spend a lot of time in water. They hunt water animals such as fish and frogs.

Raccoons mate in January or February. Females give birth about 63 days later. They have three to six kits.

Kits live on their own
after about a year.
Most raccoons live less
than five years in the wild.

Trash Eaters

Look out for your wild
neighbors. Lock up trash cans
to keep raccoons out.
Never go near raccoons.
Help wild animals stay wild.

Hands-On Activity: Animal Tracks

Do raccoons live in your neighborhood? Find out! Become an animal track expert. Explore your neighborhood or yard with an adult. Grab a notebook and a pencil, or bring a camera.

Look for animal tracks in the soil or the snow.
Look for muddy paw prints near trash cans and buildings.
Draw the tracks in your notebook, or take a photo.
Do they look like this? ⟶
If so, they are raccoon tracks!

Glossary

den—a place where a wild animal may live

kit—a baby raccoon

mammal—a warm-blooded animal that breathes air; mammals have hair or fur; female mammals feed milk to their young.

mate—to join together to produce young

nocturnal—active at night and resting during the day

wild—an area that has been left in its natural state

Read More

Johnson, Angelique. *Raccoons.* Pebble Plus: Nocturnal Animals. Mankato, Minn.: Capstone Press, 2011.

Roza, Greg. *Your Neighbor the Raccoon.* City Critters. New York: Windmill Books, 2012.

Rustad, Martha E. H. *Raccoons.* Bullfrog Books: My First Animal Library. Minneapolis: Jump!, 2014.

Internet Sites

FactHound offers a safe, fun way to find Internet sites related to this book. All of the sites on FactHound have been researched by our staff.

Here's all you do:

Visit *www.facthound.com*

Type in this code: 9781491420874

Super-cool stuff!   Check out projects, games and lots more at **www.capstonekids.com**

Critical Thinking
Using the Common Core

1. What do raccoons eat? (Key Ideas and Details)

2. What is a den? Where do raccoons build their dens? (Craft and Structure)

Index

Word Count: 184
Grade: 1
Early-Intervention Level: 18